BELIEFS:

A Workbook for Change

by

Dr. Jeremy Lopez

BELIEFS: A Workbook for Change

By Dr. Jeremy Lopez

Copyright © 2020

Published by Identity Network

P.O. Box 38213

Birmingham, AL 35238

www.IdentityNetwork.net

ENDORSEMENTS

"You are put on this earth with incredible potential and a divine destiny. This powerful, practical man shows you how to tap into power you didn't even know you had." – Brian Tracy – Author, *The Power of Self Confidence*

"I found myself savoring the concepts of the Law of Attraction merging with the Law of Creativity until slowly the beautiful truths seeped deeper into my thirsty soul. I am called to be a Creator! My friend, Dr. Jeremy Lopez, has a way of reminding us of our eternal

'I-Am-ness' while putting the tools in our hands to unlock our endless creative potential with the Divine mind. As a musical composer, I am excited to explore, with greater understanding, the infinite realm of possibilities as I place fingers on my piano and whisper, 'Let there be!'" – Dony McGuire, Grammy Award winning artist and musical composer

"Jeremy dives deep into the power of consciousness and shows us that we can create a world where the champion within us can shine and how we can manifest our desires to live a life of fulfillment. A must read!" – Greg S. Reid – *Forbes* and *Inc.* top-rated Keynote Speaker

"I have been privileged to know Jeremy Lopez for many years, as well as sharing the platform with him at a number of conferences. Through this time, I have found him as a man of integrity, commitment, wisdom, and one of the most networked people I have met. Jeremy is an entrepreneur and a leader of leaders. He has amazing insights into leadership competencies and values. He has a passion to ignite this latent potential within individuals and organizations and provide ongoing development and coaching to bring about competitive advantage and success. I would highly recommend him as a speaker, coach, mentor, and consultant." – Chris Gaborit – Learning Leader, Trainer

DEDICATION

To all seekers and lovers of the things of the Spirit who, like me, desire to grow and desire to change, this workbook is for you. May it be used to help you in the uncovering of your very own beliefs. Remember, what you believe, you will see in the world around you.   My prayer for you is that you would create an abundant life – and a beautiful world.

CONTENTS

Preface   p.1

Introduction   p.7

Analysis   p.21

Identity   p.43

The Purpose of Belief   p.55

PREFACE

elief is a very powerful force within Creation. It is so powerful, in fact, that all of life is the direct result of the beliefs we hold to. It was Jesus who declared to humanity that we will be given exactly what we believe – if we have faith and do not doubt within our hearts. The Scriptures make mention of beliefs even being the totality of life itself: "As a man thinketh in his heart, so is he." What you believe matters greatly. Your beliefs are the building blocks of your life.

However, what I know to be true is that because our beliefs are so powerful and so omnipotent, it is important that we not only know what we believe in but also that we are able to change those beliefs that are unhealthy.   If we were to be totally, brutally honest with ourselves, there are beliefs we have held to for far too long that are not only outdated but are actually quite limiting.   There are beliefs that we have outgrown. Through the powerful awakening that comes through the Holy Spirit within us, not only is it possible to examine the beliefs we hold, but it is possible to actually change those beliefs.

In my newest book *Beliefs: Make You or Break You,* I share powerful principles regarding the power of belief, and I also share candid insight and dynamic revelation regarding "truth." What is "truth?" When Jesus promised that we would know the truth and that the truth would make us free, what, exactly, was he referring to? He even promised that when the Comforter would come, we would be led into "all truth." Furthermore, it was Jesus himself who declared, emphatically, "I am the way, the truth, and the life." We know that. These statements to some degree provide us with the very basis of the faith. But, what does it all mean?

In the book, I examine the question, "What is truth?" What does it look like? Is it something that only a select few are destined to receive while all the rest are just doomed to be kept in the dark? Is this ever-elusive "truth" the same for everyone? If so, why is it that we all have different beliefs, different opinions, and various interpretations of the text of the sacred Scriptures? Suffice it to say, we are all so uniquely different. We are all so very individualistic – so fearfully and so wonderfully made.

If we are all supposed to believe the same things, see the same things, and also hope in the same things, why all the confusion where faith is concerned? Could it be that somewhere along the way, we missed something? Could it be that we have missed the entire point of the message Jesus truly shared? What if faith truly is a journey? And what if "truth" is also a journey, rather than some destination we have been called to arrive at?

What if somewhere along the way, we have missed the point about the purpose of belief?   You have heard, I am sure: "Just believe."   Although belief and faith are central to the premise of life, the idea has become almost cliché in modern religious traditions.   Believe *what*, exactly?   And what does this belief truly look like?   Are we all supposed to believe the exact same things?   In the exact same ways?

According to the false doctrines of religion, it is not enough to simply believe.   Religion demands that everyone believes the same things, exactly.   There is little room for questioning.   There is no room for change.   And when we do ask questions, religion demands that we sit down and remain quiet. There is truly nothing more deadly than religion.

As you know by now, belief just does not work that way. It is not always as simple as we would like to make it seem. We are all different. We are all learning. We are all growing.

As we grow, our perspectives change. Our beliefs change. Our vantage points change, as we continue onward in the journey of faith. What I have come to realize is, contrary to the lies of modern religion, it is not enough to simply believe. The abundant life Jesus promises demands that we believe the right things – the healthy things. For far too long you have been limited only by your limiting beliefs. It is time to change that. It is time to grow up into maturity where the faith is concerned.

INTRODUCTION

It has been said that when you change your thoughts, you change your life. Throughout the ages, much has been said about the power of thought and the power of belief. It was Jesus of Nazareth who, when speaking concerning the Kingdom of Heaven, declared that *whatsoever* things we desire, if we have faith and not doubt, we will be given exactly what we believe. Furthermore, it was Jesus who declared that all who believed on him would have everlasting life. Yes, belief is powerful, indeed. But is it possible to be sincere, yet sincerely wrong?

That is to say, is it possible to believe all the wrong things, no matter how sincerely we believe them?

When the Holy Spirit first began to inspire me with the revelation that would come to be the basis of my newest book, *Beliefs: Make You or Break You*, I found myself feeling a deep desire to better understand the realm of belief. The inner realm of belief, in fact, is the Kingdom of Heaven which Jesus spoke of continuously – the real *within*. But why is it that beliefs are so powerful? Why do our beliefs have such a dynamic effect in natural, everyday life? And if we hold to beliefs that are no longer serving us, is it possible to actually change those beliefs? If so, what does that process of change and transformation truly look like, exactly?

So much has been said throughout the years regarding the power of belief; however, rarely, if ever, has much been said about what belief truly is. In Koine Greek, the term "repentance" is *metanoia,* literally meaning "a turning in the mind." From this term, an entire religion has been founded as, for centuries, men and women, young and old, have sought to answer the call of the Gospel. "Just believe," you have so often heard it said. But what if somewhere along the way, we missed the entire point? Does change come only once? Or is change continuous? After we have experienced a moment of change and transformation, is that all there truly is?

Religious notions have relegated belief to little more than some cliché – some moment of time.   As a result, we have become proud and arrogant where our beliefs are concerned.   "I know the truth," we so often feel.   But what of all those who have different or varied beliefs, who believe something entirely differently than you do?   Are they forever damned, as religion seems to suggest?   Are they doomed to forever be kept in the dark?   If the Gospel truly is "good news," what would be so "good" about that?

Well, the "truth" of the matter is that the good news of transformation is not only possible; it is actually probable.   All throughout life, you and I are given moment after moment, opportunity after opportunity to change and to transform. Faith has always been a journey and not some point of arrival – some moment at which we can exclaim, "I have seen it all!" No, faith is more than that. Do we truly believe that a sovereign, omnipotent, transcendent God can be defined by our own finite, limiting beliefs? If so, we have missed the entire point of the Gospel.

Metanoia, in Greek, implies a change – a sort of metamorphosis if you will. It implies a transformation that goes on and on – a work that is ongoing and never stops. Throughout the years, in my own life and in years of prophetic ministry, I have seen, firsthand, how damaging certain beliefs can be. If our beliefs are truly serving as the basis of life experience, what happens when we change our minds? What happens when certain limiting beliefs no longer serve us? Do we change?

Do we change when we are presented with new truth and new revelation, or do we continue to hold to old, limiting beliefs and call it "faithfulness?" All too often, particularly where the journey of faith is concerned, we so often hold to old outdated beliefs and call it "faithfulness," continuing to defend ideas and concepts that, deep down, we don't truly even believe. We always have to be right, it seems. It has been said the definition of insanity is doing something over and over again, always expecting different results. My friend, that desire to always defend to the death the beliefs we have – even in spite of the calamity of those beliefs – isn't faithfulness; it is foolishness.

It is no wonder why the Apostle Paul spoke to the early church about the power of being transformed by the renewing of the mind – so that the will of God can be proven.   It is because our beliefs our always, always manifesting. For most, though, especially where faith is concerned, rather than being open to change, they continue to hold to limiting belief systems, unhealthy, often toxic paradigms, and continue to call it "faith."   You have been called to an abundant life – a life that truly feels good.   It is time to not only know what you believe but also why you believe it. It is time to grow up into maturity in faith.   It is time to put away childish things.

But limiting beliefs are not simply relegated to matters of faith.   No, limiting beliefs permeate all of life. From being paralyzed and gripped by fear and never being able quite able to begin the new career to suffering year after year in a dead-end relationship that stopped being fulfilling a long, long time ago, limiting, toxic beliefs are not only debilitating; they can actually be quite deadly. A limiting belief is the thief that comes to kill, to steal, and to destroy.

It is remarkable, if you truly think about it, just how much of life is often missed due to the beliefs we hold. Let us make belief much more practical where life is concerned. Let us make it personal. The reason you now find yourself living a life that feels anything but satisfying and content is because of the beliefs you are holding on to. The reason the abundant life may now seem to be so far-off and so distant is because of those old, limiting beliefs – beliefs that you have outgrown.

Like the old sweater in the closet – the one that you outgrew years ago but that is far too comfortable and familiar to throw away or to donate – there are beliefs that you have held to for a long time only because they symbolize your comfort zone. With growth comes change – a moving away from the confines and the comfort of what we have known, moving toward an even greater truth. A turning in the mind is all that is needed to lay hold of the abundant life you have been promised. The only thing standing between the life that you have and the life that you truly desire is the realm of your own belief. When awakening comes, though, and when the mind is renewed, all things become possible.

I see it time and again in my many prophetic life coaching sessions with individuals – individuals who feel so trapped in the flow of life.   I see it with men and women who have the desire to start the new business but cannot seem to get started because of deeply held fears and insecurities.   I see it in the face of the young person struggling to begin his or her life and start a path all their very own.   I see it in the face of the single mother who, suddenly, at age 45 finds herself having to start all over again.   Everything you do in life is a direct result of the beliefs you hold.

What if I were to tell you that the only thing separating you from your own dream life is your ability to change your beliefs and alter your perspective of yourself?   What if you could find that the only thing keeping you from having a satisfying, more fulfilling romantic relationship is the belief you hold to? You see, we so often view faith and belief in such spiritual, otherworldly ways that we all too often seem to forget that our beliefs are creating literally all of daily life – from the career to the home life to the relationships and everything in-between.   When you change your thoughts, you change your life.   When you change your beliefs, you begin to, in turn, change your mind.

While writing *Beliefs: Make You or Break You*, I found myself taken to the great, rich history of the faith – back to the teachings of Jesus of Nazareth. As he went about doing good and healing all that were oppressed, he shared a very powerful, quite transcendent message about the power of belief. Those early disciples who followed after him – who had forsaken all for the cause of Christ – they, too, had been given a great promise of even more to come. They were told that they would be led into all "truth." While reading the book, *Beliefs: Make You or Break You*, what you will find is the practicality of the Gospel within our lives. Yes, the Gospel is spiritual; however, it is also practical. It serves to remind us of the need to become more aware of the beliefs we hold at any given time. After all, as Jesus said, those beliefs we hold to are constantly manifesting through us and also all around us, creating the experiences of life. This workbook is designed in such a way as to be not only an accompaniment to the book but also a tool and a journal for change.

It is time to dig deeper than ever before into your own inner realm of belief in order to begin to access the abundant life you so richly deserve. It is time to not only know what you truly believe but why you believe in it. And, above all, it is time to realize that not only is it all right to change certain beliefs, it is actually the plan, the call, and the will of God to do so. The Gospel is a message of change – a change from the stagnant, limiting beliefs of religion to the unlimited nature of the new life. It is time to begin your very own new life today. It is time to look in the mirror and see what is working for you and what is no longer working. Chances are, even now, there are beliefs that you hold that, although comfortable, are stifling your productivity and growth.

What I know to be the truth and find myself reminded more and more each day is that there is always, always more. There is more of God. There is more of life. I refuse to settle. Just when I think I have seen it all, heard it all, and know it all, the glory of God shines forth and life continue to unfold around me. In the journey of faith, no one has arrived – not yet, at least.

SECTION ONE

ANALYSIS

Change begins with analysis and introspection - especially change where belief is concerned. It is no wonder, really, why Jesus compared the Kingdom of Heaven to treasure in a field and to a pearl of great price. Beliefs are priceless. Within each belief lies the power of the Godhead to create. You and I are always creating *something*, according to our beliefs.

In the sixteenth chapter of the Gospel according to Mark, Jesus speaks of the signs that will follow after those who believe. He goes on to make mention of the many miraculous signs and otherworldly feats that will follow the preaching of the Gospel, noting that the signs will be confirmation of the belief. What he was in fact saying was that beliefs are always manifesting. Even a lack of belief in yourself will manifest outwardly for all the world to see. Literally every belief is manifesting outwardly for all the world to see. Your life is the direct result of what you believe – what you believe about God, what you believe about life, and what you believe about yourself, most of all.

When the Apostle Paul in his letters to the early church spoke of the importance of transformation through the renewing of the mind, he was mentioning, emphatically, the power of belief and the need for the constant analysis of those beliefs. The same Paul who spoke so eloquently concerning the nature of the Christ within spoke, also, about his very own past – noting that he had go through so many changes of his own. The things that he once thought were gain, he counted as loss. Whether you realize it or not, you are the same way, and so am I. We are always changing. We are always growing. Paul relates this growth to a movement from "glory" to "glory."

Change is progressive. It is expansive. It is continuous. It never really ends. The journey of faith is not some momentary, one-time decision; rather, it is a life of constant analysis – constant growth and transformation, as the inner Christ is revealed more and more for all the world to see.

1. And I, brethren, when I came to you, came not with excellency of speech or of wisdom, declaring unto you the testimony of God.

2 For I determined not to know any thing among you, save Jesus Christ, and him crucified.

3 And I was with you in weakness, and in fear, and in much trembling.

4 And my speech and my preaching was not with enticing words of man's wisdom, but in demonstration of the Spirit and of power:

5 That your faith should not stand in the wisdom of men, but in the power of God.

6 Howbeit we speak wisdom among them that are perfect: yet not the wisdom of this world, nor of the princes of this world, that come to nought:

7 But we speak the wisdom of God in a mystery, even the hidden wisdom, which God ordained before the world unto our glory:

8 Which none of the princes of this world knew: for had they known it, they would not have crucified the Lord of glory.

9 But as it is written, Eye hath not seen, nor ear heard, neither have entered into the heart of man, the things which God hath prepared for them that love him.

10 But God hath revealed them unto us by his Spirit: for the Spirit searcheth all things, yea, the deep things of God.

11 For what man knoweth the things of a man, save the spirit of man which is in him? even so the things of God knoweth no man, but the Spirit of God.

12 Now we have received, not the spirit of the world, but the spirit which is of God; that we might know the things that are freely given to us of God.

13 Which things also we speak, not in the words which man's wisdom teacheth, but which the Holy Ghost teacheth; comparing spiritual things with spiritual.

14 But the natural man receiveth not the things of the Spirit of God: for they are foolishness unto him: neither can he know them, because they are spiritually discerned.

15 But he that is spiritual judgeth all things, yet he himself is judged of no man.

16 For who hath known the mind of the Lord, that he may instruct him? but we have the mind of Christ. (1 Corinthians 2:1-16 KJV)

We are always being searched, in some way. Even as the soul is prospering, the Holy Spirit is constantly attempting to inspire us toward a mindset that will cause all the rest of life to prosper as well. According to Paul, in his epistle to the early church at Corinth, the natural mind cannot even see or know the greater things.   This implies the dangers of the limiting beliefs we so often hold to.   For the mind to be renewed and for change to truly come, a certain sense of introspection is needed. It is time to begin to discover your own beliefs in a much different way than ever before.   It is time to begin to recognize what makes you so truly unique.

I have included for you a workbook to use as you analyze your own unique thoughts and beliefs. As you complete this section, I want to encourage you to be mindful that literally every belief has an origin. Every thought began somewhere; it did not just suddenly, magically become imparted into your mind from up above. No, every thought and every belief have a point of origin. Understanding this reminds us that not only can beliefs be changed but that change is actually healthy and beneficial in many remarkable ways.

(Answer the following statements with either "true" or "false.")

1.   "Never at any point do I ever doubt myself." (True) (False)

2.   "It's always easy for me to speak my truth to others." (True) (False)

3.   "Because Jesus is the way, I have all the answers I'll ever need." (True) (False)

4.   "I sometimes feel guilty for the decisions I make." (True) (False)

5.   "When I make a decision, I stand by it and never question it." (True) (False)

6.   "My faith is the only true, correct faith." (True) (False)

7.   "I always feel satisfied in life." (True) (False)

8.   "I make my own decisions and am never influenced by others." (True) (False)

9. "When I make up my mind, I know that I'm correct." (True) (False)

10. "I question myself more than I should." (True) (False)

11. "I sometimes feel unworthy." (True) (False)

12. "I'm not satisfied in my current relationship." (True) (False)

13. "My relationship is the relationship I'd always dreamed of." (True) (False)

14. "I never feel guilt of my past." (True) (False)

15. "My past often haunts me." (True) (False)

16. "My pastor is always right." (True) (False)

17. "My faith gives me all the answers I need." (True) (False)

18. "I get everything I want." (true) (False)

19. "My life is something I'm creating." (True) (False)

20. "Change always causes me anxiety." (True) (False)

Excellent. Well done. Chances are you are probably thinking: "Jeremy, what does this have to do with my belief?" Well, in fact, literally everything. This workbook is designed in such a way as to cause you to question. After all, it was Jesus who said that we should "Ask, seek, and knock." For far too long, you see, we have been afraid to analyze what we truly believe. This fear keeps us paralyzed and stuck in the limitations that we ourselves create.

My prayer for you, moving forward, is that as you progress through this workbook, using it as a tool and as an accompaniment to *Beliefs: Make You or Break You*, you will begin to analyze your own thoughts and beliefs in a much different way than ever before. Sometimes, "dissatisfaction" looks a lot like normal, everyday life. Sometimes, we do not even really know that more exists for us. My hope and prayer for you is that as you begin to dig a little deeper, you will be inspired by the treasures you find. There has always been a treasure within you – a pearl of great price. The Heaven you seek has always been within your very own inner realm of belief.

I want you to get in touch with the story of "You." You have always been more amazing and more interesting than you have realized or ever really given yourself credit for.   It is time to change that.   This change, though, begins by being able to tell your story – the story of you.   Whether you describe yourself as a person of faith or not and whether you are religious or not, chances are you hold some belief about God and the meaning of life.   Using the space provided, I want you to begin to tell your story.   What does faith mean to you? How has faith helped you to overcome some of those many obstacles in your past?   The purpose of this is to remind you of just how far you have come.   As you are sharing your story, I want you to not only remember those many moments of your life that have helped to shape who you are, but I want to encourage you to begin to see the role that you have played in writing your very own story. Consider this your "testimony:"

SECTION TWO

IDENTITY

As you read my newest book *Beliefs: Make You or Break You*, what you will find is that life is filled with moments of change – moments of transformation. All throughout life, by a unique and loving, divine design, we are always given opportunity after opportunity to change not only our lives but, also, our own minds. There is nothing more heavenly than change. As I share within the book, if the scenery stops changing, it is a sure sign that we are not really going anywhere. Scenery changes only when we are moving forward.

Somewhere along the way, where faith and belief are concerned, we parked on the side of the roadway and set up camp, thinking to ourselves, "I've seen it all" or "I know it all." This is where pride and arrogance come into play, as we begin to feel that our beliefs are somehow superior to the beliefs of others – that we have arrived at all "truth." It just does not work that way, though. There is always so much more to see and to discover. Faith, after all, is a journey.

All throughout the journey of life, though, there are turning point – moments of decision. In the rush of life, it can be quite easy to miss these moments if we are not careful. As life is happening all around us, it can be so easy to forget, in the moments, that life is also happening for us. When moments are recognized, change becomes even more possible. By learning to recognize the role that we have been given to play within the creation of our own life experiences, we not only gain greater confidence but also greater clarity of what we truly desire. I felt inspired by the Holy Spirit to include this section because, as you read *Beliefs: Make Your or Break You*, it is important that you recognize the role that you have been called to play within your own life. You have been cast in your very own starring role.

I want to journey with you as you recall some of your very own "turning points." I want you to remember and recall some of the pivotal moments that helped to define and shape you into the amazing person you are today.   Often times, change comes through the pain of life. Whereas, at other times, change comes through our own innate desire for a greater, more abundant life.   Through it all, though, it can be so easy to forget that we have always been given choices – options, if you will.   As you examine some of those many turning points within your own life, allow yourself to see the role that you played in all of them.

In a separate journal or notebook or using the "Notes" section in the back of the workbook, describe your family life, growing up.   What was the family

dynamic like?   Was there closeness?
Was it tumultuous and painful?

Describe your very first romantic
relationship.   How did it feel?   How
did it end?   Describe other romantic
relationships you have experienced
throughout your life, describing how
those relationships helped to form your
current beliefs regarding relationships.

If you were raised to be a person of faith
or were raised in a specific religion, how
did that religion serve to shape your
worldview?   How have your beliefs
changed throughout the years, where that
faith or religion is concerned?   Did you
change religions or find a new church or

stop going to church altogether? If so, please explain.

Describe in detail the dynamic with your family now. Is there closeness now? Have any of those family relationships become strained throughout the years? If so, describe what you feel to be the reasons for the tension.

If you are currently employed, or self-employed, describe in detail how and when you first knew that you wanted the job that you currently have? Would you say that you have a career you are passionate about? Why or why not?

Financially speaking, where the job or career is related, do you feel that you are making income suitable for the work that you provide?   If not, please explain.

In detail, describe the relationship dynamic to your co-workers and to those around you in the work environment. Also describe your relationship dynamic to those over you in the workplace. Have there ever been times in which you were made to feel inadequate or less-than?   If so, describe the experiences surrounding those moments.

If you are now in a current romantic relationship or a marriage, what, in your view, is the best part of the relationship? What are the stresses that you find most in the relationship? When disagreements or arguments arise, what causes them, typically?

As you will see as you read the book *Beliefs: Make You or Break You*, often, in life, change comes when we least expect it. So often, we are not even aware of the fact that we are changing – that we are growing. Through the moments of life, you and I are constantly being led toward greater truth and toward greater awareness of who we truly are. In a world that so desires to program us and condition us to be a certain way, believe a certain way, think a certain way, and even look a certain way, individuality is often considered to be a liability rather than a strength. What I pray you begin to find, though, is the understanding that all throughout the journey of your very own life, you have been given your very own turning points. Recognizing these moments of change is crucial is you are to ever heal and be able to move forward in all areas of your life. In closing this section, answer "True" or "False" to the following statements:

1. "I had a role to play in every turning point in my life." (True) (False)

2. "Even in painful moments, I've always had a say." (True) (False)

3. "Growing up, my family did the very best they could." (True) (False)

4. "I blame my family for the way things have happened." (True) (False)

5. "I often blame co-workers for strife at work." (True) (False)

6. "My marriage is what I make it." (True) (False)

7. "I have a right to change my mind - and my beliefs." (True) (False)

8. "I often feel I've disappointed my family." (True) (False)

9. "My beliefs are my very own." (True) (False)

10. "When I change my mind, I do so with confidence." (True) (False)

11. "When I change my mind, I'm fearful of what others might think." (True) (False)

12. "I easily share my opinions with others." (True) (False)

13.   "I agree with everything my family believes." (True) (False)

14.   "My beliefs aren't always right." (True) (False)

15.   "Just because someone thinks differently, doesn't mean they're wrong. (True) (False)

16.   "It's my job to convert others to share in my beliefs." (True) (False)

17.   "My faith grows as life happens." (True) (False)

18.   "I've never been a victim of my life." (True) (False)

19.   "My life is what I choose for it to be." (True) (False)

20.   "When I change my mind, I do so with confidence." (True) (False)

You see, all throughout life, in the midst of life happening, there are still moments of decision – moments in which we actually do have a very real say in matters.   Sure, it may not always seem like it. However, even in the midst of changes, we are being given the opportunity to analyze what we think, what we feel, and what we believe. You deserve more credit than you have given yourself, and you have come a long, long way.   My prayer for you is that you would begin to realize that rather than always having to be right, you will begin to enjoy the journey of life for just what it truly is – a marvelous adventure.

SECTION THREE

THE PURPOSE OF BELIEF

As you begin this final section, I invite you to take a moment to center and to ground yourself with prayer or meditation or through visualization. In this section, not only are you going to become more aware of what you truly believe, but you are going to, in turn, begin to use those beliefs to build the life of your dreams. Today, as you begin this section of the workbook, using it as a tool for your own analysis and also as an accompaniment to my new book *Beliefs: Make You or Break You*, you are going to begin to see that not only have your beliefs always, always controlled the outcome of your life but that those same beliefs possess the power to create *any* future you so desire. Yes, you have always had much more power than you have realized. And, yes, the power that works in you is greater than the power within the world.

I hope and pray by now that you have begun to take stock in all matters of your life, realizing even more that the beliefs you have held to, at times, have not served you as well as at other times. I hope and pray that you now realize just how truly powerful the realm of belief is. The Kingdom of Heaven within you –

the Christ in you – is your truest, most authentic identity. It always has been, really. It always will be.

Often times, where our beliefs are concerned, we not only forget that change is possible, but we forget even more that we have actually been *called* to change. Right now, even as you read these words, all of life is moving around you. The seasons change. Day becomes night. Hours upon the clock begin to pass by, signaling the close of a day and the beginning of another. When we refuse to change, we refuse to participate in the movement of life. To refuse to change is to refuse to truly live.

I want to close our time together by asking you a very real, very personal question – a question that only you can answer for yourself. What would you do if you could truly realize that your beliefs hold the power to create any life you dream of?   Imagine it for a moment. Let it sink in much more deeply.   That is not some motivational cliché; it is the truth of the Kingdom of Heaven.

What would it be like if you woke up each day knowing that you could have anything and everything you desired? That you could live a life that not only feels good but that feels very good? What would that life look like for you? The only thing keeping you from that life is what you believe about yourself.

You see, so often, we feel we have all the answers to the all the questions about God.   Religion always seems to have some   canned,   scripted,   rehearsed response   to   every   question   it   ever receives.   Those answers about God are so cliché that they are often laughable, at best. And, at worst, they are deadly. To some degree, you have your belief about God and the meaning of life. Somewhere along the way, though, you stopped believing in yourself. You stopped realizing that you have a right to explore what you believe. You have a right to question and to analyze. Jesus said that those who seek will find.

In this section, as you read these words, I want to take you on a guided journey of visualization into your very own bright future. As you read these words, I want you to imagine and to dream. Allow your imagination to work. Feel the sights and the sounds of those inner, mental images as you think of your future life. The truth of the matter, my friend, is that you have never really been as "stuck" as it may feel like.   You have never been as powerless or out of control as it might seem.

You see, one thing that I know beyond the shadow of any doubt is that the life we live today does not have to be the life we live tomorrow.   In fact, it does not even have to be the life we live tonight – or five hours from now.   Everything can change in an instant – in a passing moment of time.   When we change the mind, we change life itself.   Change begins with a vision.

Together, we have journeyed into the remarkable story of "You" – a story so uniquely personal and so individualistic that no other person has been able to tell the tale quite like you.   You have always been so strong.   You have always had those remarkable beliefs.

And you have always grown - even when you may not have always realized it. There is still so much more of life, though. There is more to see, to enjoy, and to experience.

1. Verily, verily, I say unto you, He that entereth not by the door into the sheepfold, but climbeth up some other way, the same is a thief and a robber.

2 But he that entereth in by the door is the shepherd of the sheep.

3 To him the porter openeth; and the sheep hear his voice: and he calleth his own sheep by name, and leadeth them out.

4 And when he putteth forth his own sheep, he goeth before them, and the sheep follow him: for they know his voice.

5 And a stranger will they not follow, but will flee from him: for they know not the voice of strangers.

6 This parable spake Jesus unto them: but they understood not what things they were which he spake unto them.

7 Then said Jesus unto them again, Verily, verily, I say unto you, I am the door of the sheep.

8 All that ever came before me are thieves and robbers: but the sheep did not hear them.

9 I am the door: by me if any man enter in, he shall be saved, and shall go in and out, and find pasture.

10 The thief cometh not, but for to steal, and to kill, and to destroy: I am come that they might have life, and that they might have it more abundantly.

11 I am the good shepherd: the good shepherd giveth his life for the sheep. (John 10:1-11 KJV)

There is so much to be said about the abundant life you have been promised –

the life that awaits you on the other side of all those limiting beliefs you are holding on to. It is no secret, really, that God wants the best for His sons and daughters. We know how He desires to give good gifts to them that ask. What we often forget, though, is that it is our own limiting beliefs that rob us, and that come as thieves, to kill and to destroy us. Your limiting beliefs and feelings of inadequacy have robbed you of the life that you truly deserve for far too long. It is time to reclaim your power and lay hold of the abundant life of your dreams by changing those limiting beliefs.

When awakening comes and when the eyes of understanding become enlightened, then and only then, do we move from the place of limitation to the place of abundance. To lay hold to this abundant life, though, you must stop robbing yourself.   You must begin to gain greater beliefs – beliefs that replace those old, limiting beliefs of self-doubt. You will never be able to experience the rich and abundant life of satisfaction of peace, love, joy, and contentment without, first, replacing the limitation.

You deserve a life that feels good.   You deserve a life filled with abundance, joy, prosperity, and all of the many, many things that make life upon Planet Earth so wonderful.   You deserve the relationship of your dreams.   You deserve the career that is satisfying – the career that brings financial security and peace of mind.   You deserve to have a life of satisfaction.   You deserve all of these things.   And these things exist for right now.   It is all on the other side of side of your beliefs.

So, now, I would ask.   What does your future look like?   What does the abundant life look like as you envision it? What does the relationship look like? What does all of that life entail?   You are the only one who can answer the questions for yourself.   No one else can do it – only you.

The abundant life, you see, does not come through entitlement or through the false, erroneous belief that says, "My way is the only way."   No, the abundant life comes through the belief that more exists.   It comes through the understanding that in order to gain clarity and perspective, certain beliefs have to shift.   What you believe about life will ultimately dictate the outcome of your life.   What you believe about your future will directly determine your future.   It is time to replace limiting beliefs with the beliefs of the Creator. Your beliefs, truly, will either make you or break you.   If the beliefs you hold seem out of alignment with the life you desire, it is time to change those beliefs. It is time to change your mind.

NOTES

ABOUT THE AUTHOR

Dr. Jeremy Lopez is Founder and President of Identity Network and Now Is Your Moment. Identity Network is one of the world's leading prophetic resource sites, offering books, teachings, and courses to a global audience. For more than thirty years, Dr. Lopez has been considered a pioneering voice within the field of the prophetic arts and his proven strategies for success coaching are now being implemented by various training groups and faith groups throughout the world. Dr. Lopez is the author of more than forty books, including his international bestselling books The Universe is at Your Command and Creating with Your Thoughts. Throughout his career, he has spoken prophetically into the lives of heads of business as well as heads of state. He has ministered to Governor Bob Riley of the State of Alabama, Prime Minister Benjamin Netanyahu, and Shimon Peres. Dr. Lopez continues to be a highly sought conference teacher and host, speaking on the topics of human potential and spirituality.